TEACHING
as Eucharist

TEACHING
as Eucharist

Take
Thank
Bless
Break
Give

JOANMARIE SMITH

Resurrection Press
Mineola • New York

First published in March, 1999 by Resurrection Press, Ltd.

P.O. Box 248

Williston Park, NY 11596

ISBN 1-878718-44-4

Library of Congress Catalog Card Number 98-68009

Cover design by John Murello

Printed in the United States of America.

For my friend and sister Maria Harris
Remembering how "we grew up together."

Acknowledgements

I want to thank Linda Mercadante, Mary Alice Piil, and Elaine Ramshaw who vetted this manuscript for theological and liturgical as well as grammatical errors. I always want to thank Suzanne Smith, Regina Coll, Elaine Roulet, and Maria del Socorro Fragoso Nevarez for their constant support of my work.

Contents

FOREWORD

Have you ever read a book that not only surprised and delighted you but also took you on a journey to places you had not expected? A book that not only described this journey but was itself an experience of journeying? This is such a book.

In *Teaching as Eucharist* Joanmarie Smith unveils a spirituality of teaching that truly is "food for the way." Of all the compelling images we might associate with our vocation of teaching, the author invites us to see teaching as our ministry of "sacred service for the people of God." More specifically she takes us on an inner journey to recognize our teaching as a form of Eucharist, and boldly asserts that as in the action of the Eucharist, we who teach are called to *take, thank, bless, break* and *give.* Each of these five actions is probed in separate chapters.

But first, there is Chapter One, dedicated to the theme of *why* we celebrate, i.e., we celebrate "to remember." With artistic deftness the varied meanings of *anamnesis* are described and their relevance to teaching are disclosed. This chapter is the keystone of the book. It deserves to be slowly pondered, indeed, to be read many times over.

The chapters that follow focus on the five Eucharistic actions of *taking, thanking, blessing, breaking,* and *giving* in their biblical and ecclesial contexts. Chapter Two plays with the action, *take.* In it we are encouraged to consider what it means to be professed teachers. The third chapter, "Thank"—in Greek, *eucharisteo,* is the core of the book. Here is one of the deepest insights I have ever read about our identity as teachers, namely, the recognition that *who* we are and even *that* we are is a function of others, our students. How to respond to that recognition is spelled out with plentiful examples. What a simple yet profound power we have by reason of our baptism—to *bless.* There are suggestions of how to make *blessing* a part of our class meetings in Chapter Four. The section on *"breaking in order that everyone may share"* in Chapter Five helps us to notice all the different methods Jesus used to nourish the people with his teaching. I was glad to find some of my standard methods among them, and was reminded that variety is possible and necessary to "break out" deeper understandings of learnings for my students as well as for myself. In Chapter Six, we are confronted with the paradox of teaching as *giving*. Here is a lesson in humility. As much as we prepare, and as much as we invite our students to learn, we can never force them to do so. The fire of motivation ultimately has to come from within themselves. Our enthusiasm and preparation are necessary for students to learn, but they are never enough to make learning happen. We can pray, however, for the energy and creativity to imitate Jesus' giving as he offered the bread and wine to the disciples.

In many ways, the last chapter encapsulates the whole book. By urging us to see our teaching as sacramental we are led to recognize that good teaching always has at its heart an air of celebration. Teaching always involves some routine, some structure, but if we can view these through the prism of celebration, these routines might become rituals which can "lift up our hearts."

A great insight of the Christian tradition is that we co-create the world by a complex interaction of spirit and matter, of what is inside of us and what is outside. Vaclav Havel, playwright, dissident, and then President of Czechoslovakia, once declared, "salvation of this human world lies nowhere else than in the human heart, in the human power to reflect, in human meekness and in human responsibility." In this little book Joanmarie Smith shows us that the power of teaching understood as Eucharist can contribute to the salvation of the world. This is a book to be prayed, not only pondered. For those who pray it, this book is sure to become a precious companion for their journey. It already is one for me.

—GLORIA DURKA

PROLOGUE

"You call me 'Teacher' and 'Lord', and you are right for that is what I am."   (Jn 13:13)

We should not be surprised that he who came that we might have life and have it more abundantly (Jn 10:10) would most frequently be addressed as "Teacher." There can be no more life-affirming task on earth than teaching. Think of what we do. We distill and evaluate the information, skills, and values of the ages. We bring the past and present into communion for the future generations of the planet. We are saying that we treasure what humanity has bequeathed to us and that we hope to enhance the treasure. We are offering "what earth has given" and "the work of human hands" and minds have made, in the belief that it can become for all of us life-giving nourishment, food for the way.

INTRODUCTION

Teaching as..... ———————————————————

Think of some images associated with teaching: teaching as midwifery, teaching as coaching, teaching as modeling, teaching as ministry. Different images lift up different emphases in our vocation. Teaching as midwifery (a description connected with Socrates) emphasizes the delivery of knowledge, skills, and values *from within* the persons we are teaching. Teaching as coaching focuses on the motivational role we play as well as showing how to do something. "Come on, you can do it! and, this is how to do it." Teacher as role model focuses on the total impact of our lives on our students more than the information or instruction we offer. Seeing our teaching as ministry, as sacred service for all the people of God, we shape our teaching according to the prophetic, priestly, and political ministry of Jesus. Of course, these images are not mutually exclusive.

Teaching as Liturgy _____

A subset of teaching as ministry is teaching as liturgy. Or, maybe, teaching as ministry is a subset of teaching as liturgy. The meaning of liturgy is public worship and before anything else, our obligation, our vocation is to worship, to adore our God. I want to help us explore what teaching as liturgy might look like, what emphases would be cultivated, how we would recognize it. More particularly, I want to examine teaching as Eucharist which is the radiating heart of all liturgical action.

Teaching as Eucharist _____

In a world where the incarnation reinforces our conviction that God is thoroughly present, that this is a universe drenched with divinity, the Blessed Sacrament is not an exception to the rest of reality but a clue to it. And grateful worship/adoration is the most appropriate response. Moreover, since the primordial expression of that response is the Great Thanksgiving, it behooves us to shape our teaching into a form of the Eucharist. The action of Eucharist involves taking, thanking, blessing, breaking, and giving. We who teach are called to take, thank, bless, break, and give. All of us are, a royal priesthood, called out of darkness into light to proclaim God's mighty acts (1 Pet 2:9).

Praying Our Vocation _____

The following suggestions are probes to foster a prayerful meditation on our teaching vocation as Eucharist. If you have ever played Pick-Up-Sticks, you will remember that the black stick was the tool with which you could prod, push, bounce, or lever and collect the other more colorful sticks. The chapters to come are like a quiver of black sticks, tools to unearth the other more colorful sticks by your own skill. Alternatively, this book is like a priming of the pump which involves pouring water until suction is established. When you feel the connection has been made, stop pouring in the water; stop reading the book and give yourself over to the Holy Spirit in prayer.

Typically, prayer is of three kinds: meditative, discursive, and contemplative. Discursive, as the name suggests, includes all the prayers which feature conversation, words, whether they be hymns, the rosary, or the prayers at Mass. Contemplation is classically defined as a wordless basking in the experience of

God. Meditation comes from the same root as medicine. Both medicine and meditation come from an earlier word meaning to take the measure of something. I like to think of meditating as pondering, as saying, "hmmmmm" while metaphorically stroking one's chin.

There appears to be some deep structure in the practice of religion that promotes all of life. The etymology of salvation and salve, the relation of holy to health and wholeness are vestiges of this structure. The insight that we become like that which we study goes back as far as Pythagoras in the sixth century B.C.E. In our case we meditatively study the Author of All Life.

In fact, these three kinds of prayer spill over into one another. Homely but precious examples illustrate the point. Have you ever talked to a beloved infant as you washed, or fed, or changed it, only to have all the love, joy, and gratitude for this precious being wash over and through you, silencing you in awe? If you have, you have an image of contemplative prayer. It can surprise you in the midst of discursive prayer. If you have ever studied a picture of a person you love, or pored over their words in a letter and found yourself framing a conversation with that person in your heart or mind, or being overwhelmed into wordless wonderment (contemplation) at this gift in your life, you have some sense of the three kinds of prayer and how they wash in and out of one another. When I say that this book is for meditating on our vocation to teach as Eucharist, it is my hope that it will foster your moving in and out of the different prayer forms.

Words, Words, Words _____

Considering this is a book about an action, you may be surprised to find a fascination with words throughout—their history, their implications, and their associations. But words bear a history as revelatory as the peoples that coined them. "[They] show marks of internal use; [they] contain their own inner conversation."[1] Carefully considered they enable us to unearth insights and suggestions we might not have considered from a cursory reading. On the other hand, the purpose of such unearthing is to lead us to action, in this case to pray and teach as eucharist.

Do this... _____

Meditation has another function besides leading us

into more intimate kinds of prayer. In a sense, it takes *our* measure. It provides a gauge by which to evaluate ourselves in light of our meditative object. It is not enough to meditate on the Lord, or say "Lord, Lord," one must do the will of God (Mt 7:21; Lk 6:46). Meditating on our teaching vocation in terms of the Liturgy of the Lord's Supper tells us what to do. "Do this," Jesus said: take, bless, thank, break, and give.

Bishop Elia Peters of India during a retreat some years ago, made the case that what we are to do "as a remembrance of him" was not to *recite* the words but, throughout our lives, to *perform* the actions of taking, thanking, blessing, breaking, and giving. At the time, I thought it was a wonderfully original but perhaps heterodox reading of the scripture. I was happy, therefore, to discover the Bishop's insights supported by scholarship. New Testament scholar, Joachim Jeremias, makes the same case in *The Eucharistic Words of Jesus*. It is evident from the Greek construction that the beseeching of Jesus, "do this as a remembrance of me" ".... is not referring to the recital of the words but to the ritual, the actions involved."[2] Nor is the Eucharist to be collapsed into the words of consecration. The Eucharistic Liturgy extends from the entrance hymn to the final blessing and dismissal.

The Gospel of John indicates that the actions have wider application than those dealing with taking, blessing, thanking, breaking and giving bread and wine. The Fourth Gospel substitutes the washing of the disciples' feet at the point in the Last Supper where the other gospel writers describe the eucharist as we most often think of it. But again, Jesus enjoins the disciples, "Do this."

> *You call me Teacher and Lord, and you are right, for that is what I am. So if I have washed your feet, you also ought to wash one another's feet. For I have set you an example, that you also should do as I have done to you....If you know these things, you are blessed if you do them.* (Jn 13:12b-15, 17)

The towel and bowl are eucharistic symbols. If we cannot confect the bread and wine into the body and blood of Christ, we can wash one another's feet—and we can teach! And we can believe that the presence of Christ will be disclosed. Everything in our sacramental theology confirms that conviction, grounded as it is in the doctrine of the Incarnation.

A Sacramental Universe _____

One of the first questions the old catechisms asked was, "Where is God?" And the answer was and still is, "Everywhere." But how can that be? In the chair I am sitting on? In the book I am reading? "Everywhere." Thomas Aquinas' description of that presence is one that I have always found most helpful. He says:

As the sun is present to the lighted air so long as it is lighted, so is God present to whatever is so long as it is. But, be-ing (is-ing) is innermost in each thing and present within all things...hence it must be that God is in all things and innermostly.

(Summa Theologica I, q8, a1.)

Any illumination that remains after switching off all artificial light is the presence of the sun. Just so, is God the "is-ing" of anything that is.

The work of Gabriel Marcel clarifies what Thomas says. During World War I, Marcel, an ambulance driver was often required to give to the wives, parents, siblings, the terrible news of the death of their loved one. He had a dossier of information on each of the men killed in action. But he soon realized that the agonizing grief suffered by those to whom he gave the dreadful information did not correspond to anything in the dossiers he held. It was not their size or weight, the color of their eyes or hair, their education or even their name that they missed. It was the unbearable loss of their being, their is-ing. This story that communicates to me the impact of Thomas' insight: As lighted air indicates the presence of the sun, so does anything and anyone that IS indicate the presence of God as the is-ing or God-ing of that thing. The insight is captured in Augustine's words, "God is more me than I am myself," (Augustine, *Confessions,* Bk III, 1 Chap. 6, 11).

The realization of the immanence of God precedes our recognition of the Incarnation. The omnipresence of God was a prehistoric intuition. Even then the saturation of the cosmos with the Deity was not believed to exhaust the Godhead. God was immanent, yes, but God also transcended the universe. Transcendence by definition includes a flushing through and going beyond.

Perhaps there is no greater book on the omnipresence of God than the Book of Psalms—the great prayerbook of all Jews and Christians. The briefest scanning of the Psalms reveals that while many of the psalms directly and unequivocally address the Godhead, many others are addressed to ourselves, to other people, including our enemies, to gates and doors, to all the elements, to mountains, to sea monsters and creeping things. Yet, apparently, they are all prayers; they are all directed toward God!

The doctrine of the Incarnation puts a new spin on the presence of God. God is not simply present as the *is* of anything that is but is present in the flesh, in the stuff of anything that is. We know now that "stuff," all "stuff" is always potentially revelatory of Deity. Our entire sacramental system flows from this awareness.

Remember the simple description of a sacrament? "An outward sign instituted by Christ to give grace." But there are two kinds of signs, those which are apart *from* that which they signify and those which are a part *of* that which they sign. There are the signs along the roadway that point towards the upcoming freeway. Then there are the signs along the freeway that tell you where you are. More and more, theologians are characterizing the sacraments as signs that are *a part of*. Note the description in the "Quiet Revolution in Sacramental Understanding":

...as the movement from seeing the sacraments as religious rites through which God breaks into our

otherwise secular lives to perceiving the sacraments
as profound symbols of God's living presence in all
of life.[3]

In some ways the sacraments resemble birthdays
and anniversaries in that we select a day of the year
and frontload it with celebratory rituals of a life or
event which, if the celebration is authentic, we revel in
everyday. On the other hand, birthdays and anniversaries do not begin to approach the phenomenon that
occurs in the celebration of a sacrament especially the
Eucharist, the Blessed Sacrament. The difference
hinges on the concept of remembrance.

One

IN REMEMBRANCE

*For I received from the Lord what I also handed on to you, that the Lord Jesus on the night when he was betrayed took bread, and when he had given thanks, he broke it and said, "This is my body which is for you. Do this **in remembrance** of me." In the same way also the cup, after supper, saying, "This cup is the new covenant in my blood. Do this, as often as you drink it, **in remembrance** of me."*

(1 Cor 11:23-25)

Saint Paul's account of the eucharistic liturgy is the earliest one we have. Scholars date this letter to the Corinthians around the year 54, that is, only a few decades after the death and resurrection of Jesus. In fact, in all of the letters of St. Paul, these are the only words of Jesus that Paul quotes directly. It is the only action of Jesus that Paul describes other than his death and resurrection. Without the gospels and other writings of the early Church we would not know anything of Jesus' birth, the miracles of his public life or his teaching in parables. Paul's recording of the event underscores the centrality of the eucharistic liturgy to the first Christian communities. They were "remembering to do" as Jesus asked.

Anamnesis which we translate as remembrance, is the doctrinal linchpin that holds together all we believe about the Eucharist. The word is Greek, but the concept is Semitic and it is a concept for which we don't have an exact equivalent. The Hebrew for *anamnesis,* remembrance is *zikkaron* and means re-present, but in the sense of "making something present again." The use of the term at the Last Supper parallels the words of God in Exodus: "This day (the day of Passover) shall be a day of remembrance for you. You shall celebrate it as a festival to the Lord; throughout your generations you shall observe it as a perpetual ordinance." (Ex 12:14)

The Passover celebration which gives us the form of the Eucharist is triggered by the youngest child's question, "Why is this night different from all other nights?" (Ex 12:26). Then the memorial begins. The prayer leader recites the great works of God as Moses directed them to do.

We were slaves of Pharaoh in Egypt and the Eternal God brought us out from there with a strong hand and an outstretched arm. Now if God had not brought out our forebears from Egypt, then even we, our children, and our children's children might still have been enslaved to Pharaoh in Egypt.[4]

But this is not simply a commemoration of what the Lord *has* done. "The saving act which God performed in the historical past becomes in the Passover feast an abidingly present, gracious reality."[5] Jews still end their Passover feast with the words, "Speedily lead your redeemed people to Zion in joy. Next year in Jerusalem!" Paul echoes this sentiment when he says to the Christians in Corinth that in the Eucharist, "You proclaim the Lord's death until he comes" (1 Cor 11:26). And so, after the Consecration, we recognize what is "a present and gracious reality" re-presented in the liturgy and we proclaim:

Christ has died, Christ is risen, Christ will come again.

And we continue the "remembering." Recall the next words in all the Eucharistic Prayers:

In the First: Father, we celebrate the *memory* of Christ your son we your people and ministers *recall* his passion.

In the Second: In *memory* of his death and resurrection, we offer you Father, this life-giving bread, this saving cup.

In the Third: Father, *calling to mind* the death your son endured for our salvation, his glorious resurrection and ascension into heaven, and ready to greet him when he comes again....

In the Fourth: Father we now celebrate this *memorial* of our redemption. We *recall* Christ's death, his descent among the dead, his resurrection, and his ascension to your right hand.

It is a valuable exercise to go through the Eucharistic Liturgy and note all the times we come upon the word "remember" or a variant of it. It is the pivot upon which the passion, death, resurrection, and second coming save us here and now, the "mechanism" by which Christ is re-presented.

But there is also God's remembering *anamnesis, zikkaron,* of us. We have some idea of what happens when we remember, make present the saving event of Jesus the Christ. But how can we know what happens when we ask God to remember. "Remember those who have died." "Remember your Church throughout the world." "Lord, remember those for whom we offer this sacrifice." "Remember those who take part in this offering, those here present and all your people and all who seek you with a sincere heart." What can this remembering mean? We can be quite sure it means more than "Don't forget."

But the main point here is, as members of a royal priesthood, we are all commissioned by Christ to do what he did—the same gestures, actions, rituals in memory of him. In our teaching ministry we are to take, thank, bless, break, and give.

What might those actions and rituals look like? In that formula: taking, thanking, blessing, breaking, giving, there is a lifetime of meditation on the vocation to teach. Our vocation is to make present the saving presence of Jesus in our time and space, to see our teaching ministry as a liturgy that proclaims the Lord until he comes again, that hastens that coming.

In the remainder of this book we will study each of the actions we are to "do" in their biblical and ecclesial contexts. Then we will explore some possibilities for "doing"—take, bless, thank, break, and give—to shape our teaching into Eucharist.

*Reflections*_____

1. Meditate on the notion of God's remembering you. Think of being re-presented in God's presence, of God's experiencing you.

2. What new insights do you receive from the Good Thief's prayer, "Remember me when you come into your kingdom" (Lk 23:42).

3. Bring to mindful prayer the students you are currently teaching. Remember especially those who seem to be having difficulties in their lives.

4. Remember those moments in your teaching career that illustrate your vocation as ministry. Thank God for these memories. Ask for more memories.

Two

TAKE

> *While they were eating, he **took** a loaf of bread, and after blessing it, he broke it, gave it to them, and said, "Take; this is my body. Then he **took** a cup and after giving thanks he gave it to them, and all of them drank from it. He said, "This is my blood of the covenant, which is poured out for many."*
>
> (Mk 14:22-24)

Mark's Gospel is the oldest, probably written around the year 70. The language of the Markan gospel is much less polished than that of Matthew, Luke and John, in that it shares a wonderful similarity to the bald Anglo-Saxon of the words of institution. One of the things that I find strangely comforting is that the English of the words of institution are so Anglo-Saxon—blunt, direct, almost to the point of crudity: Take, thank, bless, break, give. They lack the grace and musicality of the Latin *accipite, benedice, gracias agere.* Anglo-Saxon is short, punchy, unadorned.

We should not be surprised that most of our obscenities are Anglo-Saxon. It is the very bite of Anglo-Saxon that gives it its force. In 1940 Winston Churchill, appealing to the hearts and minds of the English speaking people, seemed careful to use Old English with the plain bareness for which it is noted. "We shall fight on the beaches; we shall fight on the landing grounds, we shall fight in the fields and in the streets, we shall fight in the hills; we shall never surrender." Only the word—and the idea "surrender" is foreign (Norman French).[6] This suggests that there is a directness, an unornamented deliberateness with which we ought to go about taking, blessing, thanking, breaking, and giving.

Taking Up and Taking From _____

We have two "takes" on this eucharistic action. Jesus takes up the bread and wine and enjoins the disciples to take them from him. This gives us two takes on our teaching vocation, first, the taking up of our ministry as teachers and secondly, our work in motivating our students to take from our work of human hands the life-giving nourishment we are setting before them.

Taking Up our Profession _____

Undoubtedly our first "take" should be the action of receiving and treasuring our teaching ministry, our profession. In a way, everyone is called to teach simply by reason of being human. This is obvious when we talk about parents—every child's first teachers. And who of us has not learned unforgettable lessons from children, even infants? But while all the faithful by reason of our baptism are called to the priesthood, some are called to the ministerial priesthood of word, sacraments, and pastoral leadership. So, while all are called to teach by reason of being human, some are called to exercise that ministry professionally.

Profession comes from the professing or the *taking* of vows in a religious order. During the so called dark ages in Europe, only those in monasteries were educated enough to teach or practice medicine and law. The term in its secular context does not appear in English until the middle of the Sixteenth Century. Since then profession has come to refer to any career that requires advanced learning and proposes strict ethical standards.

Professed Teachers _____

All of us may not be tenured teachers, but we are all professed teachers. Those who are retired teachers or have taken jobs in administration are like lawyers and doctors who are not currently "practicing" their profession but nevertheless are still doctors or lawyers. Perhaps it is time to pursue the connection between the profession we have "taken up" with its history in religious orders and their profession of the vows of poverty, chastity, and obedience. We are all called to live simply, to be chaste, and to obey just authority. Although most of us have not taken a vow of poverty, we know that we will never grow rich in this profession, and may not, in these days, even have security. To obey means to listen and even more importantly, to hear. Moreover, being chaste does not mean being unmarried, it means being faithful in our appropriate relationships. It is too bad that we don't have a stole-like vestment to kiss and put on each day as we go to class to remind us that our yoke is sweet and our burden light—to remind ourselves and our students of our profession.

Of course, we don't always experience the dailyness of our call, of the ministry we have taken up, as sweetness and light. We hear sympathetically and identify with the warning of James:

> *Not many of you should become teachers, my brothers and sisters, for you know that we who teach will be judged with greater strictness. For all of us make many mistakes.* (Jas 3:1-2)

In fact, on some days, we may think one of those mistakes may have been to take up this ministry of teaching. James gives us some indication that he was having a "bad day" when he wrote that. In a long, and some might even say tedious list of exhortations, this is the only personal note. It is the only place where he identifies with the problems he is excoriating. Who of us cannot identify with James' bad day. When I look back to some moments teaching the fourth grade in Brooklyn, I certainly can. And I still have those kinds of days teaching adults in a seminary! (Are there any teachers who don't enjoy snow days as much as their students?) Obviously, however, if we are still in the teaching ministry the good days far, far outnumber the bad days.

Still, on some days we need help to keep on keeping on. How can we nourish commitment to this call to our ministry? Margaret Farley in her book on commitment has a number of suggestions. One is focused on "remembrance." She says remembering is a way of nourishing our commitment. Farley encourages us to remember the original vision. Though we may no longer see what first compelled our commitment, it is still there.[7] Just because we no longer experience the heady moments (or years) of relishing our ministry as gift—to ourselves as well as to the Church in the world—does not mean it is less gift.

St. Thomas Aquinas says that God leads us by desire (*Summa Theologica* I, q.105, a.4, ad 1). Reflect on what initiated that desire to teach. In most cases it will be the experience of being taught and liking it. Most of us can recall teachers who inspired us. For many of us a teacher was our first love beyond the family. We usually term such love affairs "crushes." To the extent that such crushes have the effect of reshaping our lives, perhaps the term is apt. As we get older, we can be dazzled by the sheer brilliance of a teacher as she or he choreographs a discipline such that we are caught up in the dance and find ourselves gracefully exercising the steps.

Recalling that original vision energizes our capacity to experience it again. An Amazing Grace! "How precious did that grace appear, the hour I first believed."

When were you first aware of your call to teach? What were the circumstances in which the Church or civil leaders elected you to minister among them? How was your vocation tested by these representatives of the people? Remember the licensing or certification which is confirmation of the call. Remembering—making present those moments, that original vision—can give us the juice to continue to teach in joyful hope for the coming of our savior, Jesus Christ.

Reflections _____

1. Using a concordance which lists all the words in the Bible, look up "take" and reflect on other uses for the term, e.g. "He took our infirmities and bore our diseases" (Mt 8:17). "[The Kingdom of God] is like leaven that a woman took..." (Lk 13:21). "We toiled all night and took nothing" (Lk 5:5).

2. Meditate on what "take" means in each context.

3. What is God revealing in this context?

4. How does this revelation apply to your life? How does it apply to your teaching?

5. Play with other possible meanings of "take" by adding prepositions, e.g. take in, take on, take account of, take off, take out, and so on.

Three

THANK

*Then he took a loaf of bread, and when he had given **thanks**, he broke it and gave it to them, saying "This is my body, which is given for you. Do this in remembrance of me." And he did the same with the cup after supper, saying, "This cup poured out for you is the new covenant in my blood."*

(Lk 22:19-20)

"Thank" is the nucleus of liturgy; this is where the weight is. This is the verb that gives the entire pattern its name: in Latin, *agere gracias*; in Greek, *eucharisteo*. This suggests that gratitude is to be an abiding attitude toward life—and death. Our earliest socialization begins with petition and gratitude. "Say, 'Please.'" "Say, 'Thank you.'" We find ourselves gravitating to those people in our lives who seem to exhibit this attitude. They appreciate and relish living. Life appreciates for them, that is, grows in value. It is hard to resist this stance towards life. If we bring this perspective to our teaching it invariably infects our students. They

41

begin to see us as treasuring our vocation to them and to our subjects. If we communicate to them our awe at being able to influence the next generation, they cannot help but be caught up in this engagement to promote the coming reign of God. I find myself much less hesitant about saying to my students, "I can't believe how blessed I am to be here, to be teaching you." Sharing my astonishment and joy at my role in their lives has generated a mutual reverence among us and earnestness to repair the world, a work to which we are all called.

Thankful for our Students _____

But if the focus of the liturgy is thanksgiving, the focus of that for which we give thanks must be our students. They are the condition of our identity as teachers. As someone cannot be a mother unless she has a child, so there are no teachers unless there are students. I am not speaking of being out of a job because of low registrations. Rather, _who_ we are and even _that_ we are is a function of others. As our existence depends upon a man and woman bringing us into being, so does every other designation that describes us depend on others. To be sister, brother, spouse, police officer, physician, friend, requires the cooperation and recognition of other persons. Let us give thanks for our students then, say grace over them. "Bless us O Lord and these your gifts whom we are about to teach." And let us thank our students.

We can say, "thank you" to them, but there are only so many times this can be verbalized before becoming vacuous. What we need is some ongoing attitude that conveys our gratitude. I suggest that attitude is one of thoughtfulness. The clue comes from the word in Anglo-Saxon that roots *both* "thank" *danke* and "think" *denke.* That source connotes the reasoning dimension of thanking which, combined with love, gives us a current notion of thoughtfulness. Think of what we mean when we describe a gift as "thoughtful." It is timely and reflects both affection and knowledge of what would please the recipient. A dictionary describes ways of expressing our thankfulness, thoughtfulness. "The showing of thought for the comfort or well being of others, as by anticipating their needs or wishes." This definition gives us something of a checklist.

How attentive are we to the physical comfort of our students during class time? Their health? Their family situations? What needs of theirs can we meet beyond the obvious one of motivating them to learn? What wishes can we fulfill if we think creatively enough?

As we go through this checklist a problem may arise. If we "ought always and everywhere give thanks to God" how can we be grateful for the deplorable conditions we sometimes find among our students and certainly in the world at large. There are students whose physical limitations seem to preclude comfort or whose family situations appear to defy our ability to meet their obvious, perhaps tragic needs. Can we give thanks for the atrocities in Bosnia, for the suffering of the Third World (actually the Two Thirds World), for the suffering in our families, for the suffering in our own lives? Not easily. And here at the center of our teaching as liturgy, as well as the liturgical celebration of the Eucharist, lies a profound mystery. After the initial liturgy, Jesus enters his agony in the garden, and just before the ritual of institution Jesus acknowledges that he is about to be betrayed (Mk 14:18b). Yet, Jesus goes on to give thanks, *eucharisteo*.

In a recent work, Maria Harris, speaks of thanksgiving and evil as being "inextricably connected."[8] She writes insightfully of the fact that it is our recognition of the goodness that already exists in the world, that enables us to see that it is incomplete goodness, that enables us to recognize evil. Therefore, before we take action against the evils we see:

> *We must pause to give thanks for the ordinary and pervasive gifts of life. Gratitude is not only the final ritual, it's the initial one too. Paradoxically, the starting point in facing evil is not the prophetic stand against it. The starting point is the genuflection of thanksgiving.*[9]

Thus gratitude as the centerpiece of our teaching ministry has a social conscience as its upshot. "Our refusal to tolerate evil comes as a direct result of realizing that the gifts of life belong to everyone."[10] Helping our students be aware and grateful for the goodness in the universe, simultaneously makes them aware of where it needs to be completed and where it seems lacking altogether. It makes us all more thoughtful of our obligation to complete the goodness and eliminate the evil.

Reflections

1. Where do you find it easy to be grateful? Where do you find it difficult to give thanks?

At Passover, Jews thank God with a Litany of Gratitude, each phrase of which concludes *Dayenu,* "It would have been enough."

If God divided the Red Sea for us and not let us pass through it dry-shod...

"It would have been enough."

Had God sustained us in the wilderness for forty years and not fed us with manna.

"It would have been enough."

Pray a litany of persons or events in your teaching ministry for which you are grateful. Conclude each with *Dayenu* or, "It would have been enough."

2. Where do the gifts in your life make you uneasy with their lack in the lives of others? Prayerfully ask for insight into what you can do to make life less unfair.

Four

BLESS

While they were eating, Jesus took a loaf of bread, and after **blessing** it he broke it, gave it to the disciples, and said, "Take, eat, this is my body." Then he took a cup, and after giving thanks he gave it to them saying, "Drink from it all of you; for this is my blood of the covenant which is poured out for many for the forgiveness of sins." (Mt 26:26-28)

Scholars tell us that this blessing was a giving of thanks—a kind of grace (thanks) before meals where we say, "Bless us O Lord and these your gifts..." In fact, since Vatican II, only the giving of thanks and praise is mentioned in the words of consecration with the exception of the fourth Eucharistic Prayer in which the presbyter says, "When they were at supper, he took bread, _said the blessing..._" Blessing, therefore, implies a continuation of thanking. We speak of blessings in life as being those persons and events and things for which we are especially grateful. But it has also acquired the sense of hallowing and consecrating.

This double meaning is suggested in the *Catechism of the Catholic Church* when it says "Every baptized person is called to be a 'blessing' and to bless" (#1669).

We pray, of course to be a blessing in the lives of our students and our colleagues.

Being a Blessing

When people speak of blessings in their lives, we know they are characterizing someone or some circumstance as a singular manifestation of God's generosity and love. We experience blessings as gifts of divine origin. As such, we can hardly "work" on being a gift of God. But at least we can try working out those dispositions that get in God's way of fashioning us into gift. These tendencies are classically defined as pride, envy, hostility, laziness, greed, gluttony and lust. And we can assume that God wants to imbue us with the fruits of the Spirit: love, joy, peace, patience, kindness, generosity, faithfulness, gentleness, and self-control (Gal 5:22-23). In fact, we can claim these fruits as the effects of our baptism. They are blessings in our lives that make us blessings in the lives of others.

Conferring a Blessing _____

"Bless" is also etymologically related to bliss. The connection implies that we should set up an environment where our students experience bliss, where they feel blessed to be, where they experience joy. Sara Maitland in her wonderful book *A Big Enough God* calls joy the "O Wows" of life.[11]

One of the "O Wows" in life is our power to bless, again as the *Catechism* reminds us, by reason of our baptism. The ritual of blessing our students is one that we in the North Atlantic Community have failed to adopt. I mean raising our hands and making the sign of the cross over these young people. This possibility is so vivid in my mind because I recently spent time in the home of a friend in Durango, Mexico. Each night at precisely 7 p.m. we would gather in the living room before the altar and recite the rosary and other prayers. At the conclusion of these prayers we would each kneel in front of her elderly father's chair and he would bless each one of us. Often while we were praying, at least two of the grandchildren would be gambling around us—Carmelita one and a half and Cesar, a precocious two-and-a-half year old. On my last night there, as my friend, Socorro, and I were about to board the bus for Mexico City, two-and-a-half year old Cesar (admittedly, at the prompting of his mother), blessed me with the same words and the same ritual as his grandfather. On my next trip, I expect Carmelita to preside. They are being educated to their priestly powers.

If we teach in a public institution, explicitly Christian gestures may not be possible. But we can wish our students well in a way that they will know they are being blessed. On the other hand, those of us whose situations allow us to be explicit may not be taking advantage of that opportunity. Picture yourself blessing your students at the end of each day or as they leave for the weekend. In so doing you echo the letter of Peter:

We are a chosen race, a royal priesthood, a holy nation, God's own people in order that we may proclaim the mighty acts of the One who called us out of darkness into the marvelous light. Once we were not a people, but now we are God's people; once we had not received mercy, but now we have received mercy. (1 Pet 2:9-10)

As we dismiss a class, a simple blessing such as marks the dismissal at Mass is appropriate. "May the blessing of almighty God, the Father, Son, + and Holy Spirit, come upon you and remain with you forever." I myself like the solemn or threefold blessings which you may want to save for the end of the week. They might go something like this:

By reason of your baptism you are a holy people, God's people.

May God give you the energy and insight to live out your baptism. **R. Amen.**

May each day find your faith in God stronger and stronger. **R. Amen.**

May you be filled with joy and peace this day (this weekend, etc.) and all your days. **R. Amen.**

And may almighty God bless you, the Father, and the Son, + and the Holy Spirit. **R. Amen.**

Reflections _____

1. What specific blessings do you associate with your teaching vocation?

2. What dispositions work against your being gift to your students? What gifts of the Spirit can you claim to overcome these obstacles?

3. What gifts of the Holy Spirit do you recognize in yourself or that others have noted that contribute to your being a blessing in the lives of your students?

4. Using the pattern of the solemn or threefold blessing, compose a blessing that is particularly fitting for your class.

5. "Follow your bliss," is an expression attributed to Joseph Campbell. What constitutes your bliss and how do you follow it?

Five

BREAK

*Taking the five loaves and the two fish, he looked up to heaven, and blessed and **broke** the loaves and gave them to the disciples, and the disciples gave them to the crowds.*   (Mt 14:19)

*And he took the seven loaves, and after giving thanks he **broke** them and gave them to the disciples to distribute; and they distributed them to the crowd.*
(Mk 8:6)

*When he was at table with them [the disciples from Emmaus], he took bread, blessed and **broke** it and gave it to them....Then they told [the Apostles and their companions in Jerusalem] what had happened on the road, and how he had been made known to them in the **breaking** of the bread.*   (Lk 24: 30, 35)

It becomes obvious that the "breaking of bread" in the

feeding of the multitude stories is an intimation of the Eucharist. As if to underscore this point, after that miracle story is recorded in John's gospel, Jesus tells the crowd:

> *I am the living bread that came down from heaven. Whoever eats of this bread will live forever; and the bread that I will give for the life of the world is my flesh.* (Jn 6:51)

Perhaps the "Breaking of Bread" expression evolved as the description of the Eucharist in a way similar to that of "Mass" which also refers to a single element of the entire ritual—the dismissal. *The Catechism of the Catholic Church* lists more than fifteen ways of referring to what we do "in remembrance of him." It gives primacy of place to "Eucharist," "Lord's Supper," and "The Breaking of Bread." The Mass is the last designation it cites. One of my favorite expressions (after Eucharist, of course) is "Holy Things" (#1328-1332).

In any case, when we read a summary of the life of the first Christians after Pentecost, we know immediately how central the Eucharist was to that life.

> *They devoted themselves to the apostles' teaching and fellowship, **to the breaking of bread** and the*

*prayers....Day by day, attending the temple together and **breaking bread** in their homes, they partook of food with glad and generous hearts.* (Acts 2:42, 46)

"Break" in this context cannot mean you should break your students. Nor can it mean that you should allow yourself to be broken, or burn out. It is the breaking that is done in order to share. It is the break captured in the exclamation, "Let's break out the champagne." This breaking is intimately connected with the next action of our liturgy: Give. Breaking the bread makes it possible to give each disciple a piece. All share equally in the communion—even if the size of the pieces vary.

As we meditate on the application of breaking in order that everyone may share, we inevitably think of the necessity of breaking up a subject or topic to make it palatable to our students. Our students do not learn at the same pace or in the same way. We break open our subjects and methods to give everyone another kind of "break." In preparing lectures, lessons, or plan books, we might pray that under the guidance of the Holy Spirit we can break our subject into manageable pieces and into forms where everyone will be nourished. Jesus used many different methods to nourish the people with his teaching. *Audio visuals:* children on his lap, overloaded fishing nets; *Storytelling:* The Prodigal Son (Lk 15:11-32), and The Dishonest Manager (Lk 16:1-11); *Problem Solving:* all the parables; *The Socratic Method:* "Which of these three, do you think, was neighbor to the man who fell among robbers?" (Lk 10:36), "Who do you say I am?" (Mt 16:15); *Lecturing:* Sermon on the Mount (Mt 5, 6, 7).

I have avoided mentioning the miracles but Jesus did promise that those who believed will be able to do the works he did "and even greater works than these will they do" (Jn 14:12b). Moreover, Jesus promised that with faith even as small as a grain of mustard seed we can say to a mountain, "Move from here to there, and it will move; nothing will be impossible" (Mt 17: 20b). We may have to break up the mountain and move it piece by piece, but, in any case, we are well advised to keep miracle-making in our list of teaching methods.

Reflections _____

Although there are many times that the word "break" can be found in the New Testament, the Greek verb as it is used to describe Jesus' actions with bread is not related to any of these other uses of "break." But I believe we are justified in using break idiomatically when the end product is sharing. Therefore, think of things you can break that would enhance your teaching ministry.

1. Consider "breaking out" the books that would enable you to deepen your teaching skills or deepen your understanding of your subject or your understanding of your students as subjects (as opposed to objects).

2. Can you break some habit that restricts your ability to share a vigorously healthy teacher with your students?

3. What breaks can you give your students that will enhance their capacity to share?

4. What breaks can you give yourself that will enhance your capacity to share?

Six

GIVE

*In their memoirs, which are called gospels, the apostles passed on the instructions given to them, as follows: Jesus took bread, gave thanks, and said, "Do this in remembrance of me; this is my body." In a similar manner, he took the cup, gave thanks, and said, "This is my blood." And he **gave** it to them alone.* (St. Justin, Apology 1:66.3)

Justin wrote the above to Emperor Antoninus Pius around 155 in order to defuse the sensational rumors that surrounded the meetings of Christians in the second century. Not that it did much good. We know the man today as St. Justin Martyr. He was executed by order of the emperor Marcus Aurelius who succeeded Antoninus. But it is awesome that from these early centuries of terrible persecution we have this record: "On the day we call the day of the sun, all who dwell in the city or country gather in the same place," and celebrate Eucharist from all accounts and purposes pretty much as we do today (*Apology* 1:66-67).

The Paradox of Giving _____

Jesus offers the bread and wine to the disciples and asks them to eat and drink. But he cannot make them take the offerings. He cannot make them chew or gulp and swallow. We can picture his body leaning in towards each disciple with an inviting expression on his face as he gives them a rationale for what he is asking. But in the end he is powerless before the disciples' freedom. That is the paradox of giving. Give is, as we say, a transitive verb. It requires a receiver. Which is precisely what we cannot guarantee. As teachers we have to remind ourselves of this fact. When we do, I believe our giving takes the form of motivation.

Giving as Motivation _____

I have become convinced that there are not two kinds of teaching: deductive and inductive. There is only inductive. We usually think of deductive as starting with the conclusion: H_2O = water. Then we set up a series of steps whereby this conclusion is proved. Inductive begins with the process and the students discover the conclusion. Everyone agrees that people are more likely to internalize and remember what they themselves have discovered. But in fact every conclusion must be "discovered."

And we cannot discover it for our students. Along with our inability to make horses drink after we have led them to water, is our inability to make students learn. They must teach themselves. That is what we mean by learning. I have begun therefore to think of teaching as the intentional organization of the environment in which persons can learn (teach themselves).

One of the images that informs my teaching more and more is that of Elijah teaching the Israelites who the true God is. In 1 Kings 18:20-40 the Israelites are challenged by Elijah to settle on Yahweh or Baal as their God. He sets up a teaching situation where the four hundred fifty prophets of Baal are to prepare a sacrifice for their deity. Elijah will do the same for Yahweh. Whichever Lord answers will be the true God. The prophets of Baal petition their deity for hours with no response. Then Elijah steps up to the task. Somewhat theatrically he demands that the sacrifice be soaked with water. And again. And a third time. Finally, he demands that a trench be dug around the sacrifice and filled with yet more water. (I picture him in a Groucho Marx cutaway, mustache and cigar, raising the ante, as it were, by asking for the water.) Then Elijah prays:

Answer me, O Lord, answer me, so that this people may know that you, O Lord, are God, and that you have turned their hearts back." **Then the fire of the Lord fell and consumed the burnt offering, the wood, the stones, and the dust, and even licked up the water that was in the trench.**

When all the people saw it, they fell on their faces and said, **"The Lord indeed is God; the Lord indeed is God."** (1 Kgs 18:37-40)

This scene dramatically symbolizes our teaching roles of preparation, prayer, and powerlessness. Preparation of the environment is fundamental. That includes the space of course, but does not exhaust what is meant by the environment.

Intrinsic and Extrinsic Motivation _____

Intrinsic and extrinsic motivation is another set of traditional categories found in educational literature. Most theorists agree that intrinsic motivation is the ideal. When learning itself becomes pleasurable the teacher only needs to get out of the way of the student or provide the guidance that is asked for. But all subjects do not have the same appeal, all the time, to all our students. Jesus himself was not above using extrinsic motivation. He gives a rationale for taking the bread and wine he is offering the disciples. "For this is my body, given for you." "This is the blood of the new covenant which is poured out for many for the forgiveness of sins" (Mt 26:28). "Whoever eats of this bread will live forever" (Jn 6:51). Forgiveness of sin and eternal life are compelling motivations to do (eat bread and drink wine) what on the face of it has nothing to do with either one of these actions.

We know we must get our students' attention, get them inside the tent, as it were.

The more creative among us do that Elijah-like, with flair. Some infect their students like the professor of astrophysics whose excitement is so contagious that her students are dis-eased into learning, into teaching themselves. Some are like the nursery school teacher who is able to craft every topic into a win-win learning game. Others make the subjects themselves appealing. And the subject's appeal is, "Play with me."

In the end, however, we are powerless to make students learn. Our creative preparation and execution are essential but insufficient conditions. So we must pray furiously that the fire comes. I think we must also provide the opportunity for students to pray that the fire comes. Describing to them our inability to learn for them may promote a new sense of their responsibility in the act of teaching. Of course, such insights on their part may additionally burden us as they importune us to accommodate more to their learning styles and learning curves. O happy burden!

O God, give us the energy and inventiveness to imitate the giving of Jesus to his disciples and fire our students to give themselves over to learning, to teaching themselves.

Reflections _____

1. In *Webster's Collegiate Dictionary* there are over forty definitions of "give" not including compounds, or colloquial use, or derivatives as "given." Consider how some of these other meanings could apply to your teaching as eucharist.

2. Reflect on your own education. Did you ever find yourself enjoying a subject or course that is traditionally considered boring? What precipitated

the enjoyment? Can you get any tips from this reflection for your own teaching?

3. Another way of thinking of giving is as proposing. Proposals of marriage call for attention to place and time: an aesthetically appropriate environment, a sensitivity to the ripeness of the relationship. What clues can you get for your teaching task from this image?

4. Proposals for grants from federal or private sources require a well organized rationale for whatever one is proposing. What clues can you get for your teaching task from this image?

Seven

AMEN

"Amen" the conclusion of every prayer and ritual is both an acclamation and a hope: "So be it!" and "Let it be so!". "Amen" captures the "already/not yet" character of our eucharistic teaching. If our entire life is lived in thanksgiving, according to the Eucharistic formula, we are more likely to move the not yet of our teaching into the already. Teaching as Eucharist cannot be a day job that bears no resemblance to the rest of our lives.

In the model of the liturgy given us by St. Hippolytus early in the third century, we acknowledge, "It is right to give God thanks and praise." Moreover, "Father, it is our duty and our salvation to _always and everywhere_ give you thanks through your Son Jesus Christ." Because we live in a sacramental universe, there is no _where_ that cannot be a Eucharistic altar; there is no _when_ that the Eucharistic action is inappropriate. How taking, blessing, thanking, breaking, and giving will permeate one's life is best left to the individual's prayerful meditation. But I believe that a Eucharistic *life* will be distinguished by celebration, evangelization, and communion.

Celebration _____

When authentic celebration occurs it is always a gift. But as Corita Kent was wont to say, "If you ice a cake, light sparklers and sing, something celebrative may happen." We recognize immediately the ritual Kent is describing. A pervasive celebratory stance towards existence takes advantage of every opportunity to ritualize both the commonplace and the extraordinary events of life. Rituals are the structures upon which all celebrations are fashioned. They are the patterns of actions and words upon which we hang our hope for celebration. And all rituals in which celebration comes off have a sacramental character.

Until the middle ages there was no fixed number of sacraments. St. Augustine listed over thirty rituals that he considered sacraments. Many things were regarded as sacraments including holy scripture, most devotions, and even the mysteries of our faith. The Council of Trent however settled on the number seven and described all the other "Holy Things" as sacramentals—not in the same league, but reflecting the same principle: After the Incarnation we know that finite reality can disclose and communicate the Deity; our God is Emmanuel—God with us.

The Church guides us to experience this reality through certain actions, words, and things which it designates officially as sacraments and sacramentals—realities imbued with the hidden presence of God as Paul VI described them. In its wisdom, the Church simply reflects that we are a sacralizing species. Which is to say, we are always consecrating actions, words, and things in our relationships with others. We prepare special meals to celebrate memorable occasions. We save "relics"—love letters, photos, ticket stubs. We have songs that are "our songs." We bronze and exhibit the baby's first shoes. We consecrate these moments, items, in order to celebrate the relationships they signify. There is no reason that these moments and items cannot also celebrate glimpses of God's goodness to us as the Church encourages us to do so. *The Catechism of the Catholic Church,* speaking of sacraments and sacramentals, says: "There is scarcely any proper use of material things which cannot be directed toward our salvation and the praise of God."

Evangelization _____

We no longer think of evangelizing as the attempt "to convert pagans in heathen lands." The documents of Vatican II insisted that the Church "rejects nothing of what is true and holy in religions" and further counseled us:

> To enter with prudence and charity into discussion and collaboration with members of other religions. Let Christians, while witnessing to their own faith and way of life, acknowledge, preserve and encourage the spiritual and moral truths found among non-Christians, also their social life and culture. *(The Relation of the Church to Non-Christian Religions)*

These contemporary insights move us to the original meaning of *evangelion, godspel, good news.* Like the tendency to celebrate, the inclination to share good news seems to be hard wired into human nature. Consider the joy that doctors must experience when they can report to anxious parents, "Your child is going to live," or less dramatically but still pleasurably, our happiness as teachers when we can write on an exam, "This is an excellent piece of work." It seems inevitable, therefore, that if like the Disciples at Emmaus (Lk 24:13-35) our eyes have been opened and we have known the Risen Christ in the breaking of bread, with hearts burning within us we will be forced to proclaim:

Christ has died, Christ is risen, Christ will come again!

Dying he destroyed our death, rising he restored our life, Lord Jesus come in Glory!

By his cross and resurrection, the Lord has set us free!

Communion

Jesus pleaded for us during his last supper, "Father, that they may be one even as we are one....That they may all be one...That they may be one, even as we are one....That they may be perfectly one (Jn 17:11, 21, 22, 23). This is not the oneness of identity, of being absorbed into one another. The persons of the Trinity emerge from their distinguishable relationships to each other. As the doctrine states it: "The Father is not the Son, and the Son is not the Father, nor is the Holy Spirit the Father or the Son." This central mystery of our faith reveals that Reality at its Source is communal. The Trinity offers us an image of how all reality should be—in communion, in community. It is Paul's distress at the rumors that there are divisions in the Church at Corinth that prompts him to recall the liturgy he had received from the Lord, "That on the night when he was betrayed, he took bread...." Our current media explosion assures us that there are divisions among us. In particular, the rich get richer and the poor get poorer. Paul excoriates us. "Do you despise the Church of God and despise those who have nothing?" (1 Cor 11:22). Our lives cannot be Eucharistic, therefore, if we are not actively promoting justice, "the structured struggle to share the good God's earth." [12]

Reflections _____

1. Reflect on your life outside of your teaching ministry. How might you apply the Eucharistic actions of *taking, blessing, thanking, breaking,* and *giving*?

2. Herbert Vorgrimler in his *Sacramental Theology* says:

> There are events in individual and community life that disturb and fascinate us (such as being born, common meals, sexuality, death) and therefore incline people to surround them with rites, and this way to pay attention to the deeper dimensions of their being and to give heed to the presence of God.[13]

How do you celebrate the presence of God in the events that "disturb and fascinate" you?

3. In what ways does your life proclaim your faith in God? How often do you find yourself forced to share the Good News of Jesus' passion, death, and resurrection?

4. Think of the ways the unity in diversity and equality of the Godhead can inform your passion for justice?

5. Choose a symbol of your teaching vocation and unpack it. That is, explore why this symbol captures your profession for you.

EPILOGUE

Let us go forth to love and serve the Lord.

PRAYER FOR TEACHERS

Father, all-powerful and ever-living God,
we do well always and everywhere to give you thanks
through Jesus Christ our Lord.
At the last supper,
as he sat at table with his apostles,
he offered himself to you as the spotless lamb,
the acceptable gift that gives you perfect praise.
Christ has given us this memorial of his passion
to bring us its saving power until the end of time.
In this great sacrament you feed your people
and strengthen them in holiness,
so that the human family
may come to walk in the light of one faith,
in one communion of love.
We come then to this wonderful sacrament
to be fed at your table
and grow into the likeness of the risen Christ.

Earth unites with heaven
to sing the new song of creation
as we adore and praise you for ever.
— Preface Holy Eucharist II

Endnotes

1. Lewis Thomas, *Lives of a Cell: Notes of a Biology Watcher* (New York: Viking Press, 1974), p. 132.

2. Joachim Jeremias, *The Eucharistic Words of Jesus.* trans. Arnold Ehrhardt (Oxford: Basil Blackwell, 1955), p. 161-162.

3. Robert L. Browning and Roy A. Reed, *The Sacraments in Religious Education and Liturgy* (Birmingham, AL: Religious Education Press, 1985), p. 11. See also Karl Rahner, *Theological Investigations XIV* (London: Darton, Longman & Todd, 1976), p. 166.

4. Johannes H. Emminghaus, *The Eucharist: Essence, Form, Celebration.* trans. Matthew J. O'Connell (Collegeville, MN: Liturgical Press, 1978), p. 17.

5. *Ibid.*, p. 19.

6. Robert McCrum, William Cran, and Robert MacNeil, *The Story of English* (Viking, New York, 1986), p. 62.

7. Margaret A. Farley, *Personal Commitments* (San Francisco: Harper and Row, 1986), p. 48-51.

8. Maria Harris, *Jubilee Time: Celebrating Women, Spirit, and the Advent of Age* (New York: Bantam, 1995), p. 190.

9. *Ibid.*, p. 191.

10. *Ibid.*

11. Sara Maitland, *A Big Enough God: A Feminist's Search for a Joyful Theology* (New York: Riverhead Books, 1996), p. 156.

12. Matthew Fox, *A Spirituality Named Compassion and the Healing of the Global Village and Us* (Minneapolis: Winston Press, 1979), p. vi.

13. Herbert Vorgrimler, *Sacramental Theology* (Collegeville, MN: The Liturgical Press, 1992), p. 16.

About the Author

Joanmarie Smith, the William A. Chryst Professor of Pastoral Theology at the Methodist Theological School in Ohio, is a Sister of St. Joseph (Brentwood, New York). She has her doctorate in philosophy from Fordham University. She has authored, co-authored, and edited seven books and published at least forty articles. Her most recent book, *A Context for Christianity in the 21st Century*, was published in 1995 by Thomas More Press. She uses the honorarium from speaking engagements and royalties to support a house of spiritual formation for young Zapotec lay-women in the Sierra Madre mountains of Oaxaca, Mexico.

Published by Resurrection Press

For a free catalog call 1-800-892-6657